GUIDED MEDITATION

Guided Meditations for Beginners From a Certified Reiki Healer

(Simple Mindfulness Techniques to Harness All the Benefits)

Joseph Hanso

Published by Alex Howard

Joseph Hanson

All Rights Reserved

Guided Meditation: Guided Meditations for Beginners From a Certified Reiki Healer (Simple Mindfulness Techniques to Harness All the Benefits)

ISBN 978-1-77485-069-5

All rights reserved. No part of this guide may be reproduced in any form without permission in writing from the publisher except in the case of brief quotations embodied in critical articles or reviews.

Legal & Disclaimer

The information contained in this book is not designed to replace or take the place of any form of medicine or professional medical advice. The information in this book has been provided for educational and entertainment purposes only.

The information contained in this book has been compiled from sources deemed reliable, and it is accurate to the best of the Author's knowledge; however, the Author cannot guarantee its accuracy and validity and cannot be held liable for any errors or omissions. Changes are periodically made to this book. You must consult your doctor or get professional medical advice before using any of the suggested remedies, techniques, or information in this book.

Upon using the information contained in this book, you agree to hold harmless the Author from and against any damages, costs, and expenses, including any legal fees potentially resulting from the application of any of the information provided by this guide. This disclaimer applies to any damages or injury caused by the use and application, whether directly or indirectly, of any advice or information presented, whether for breach of contract, tort, negligence, personal injury, criminal intent, or under any other cause of action.

You agree to accept all risks of using the information presented inside this book. You need to consult a professional medical practitioner in order to ensure you are both able and healthy enough to participate in this program.

Table of Contents

INTRODUCTION 1

CHAPTER 1: WHY MEDITATE? 3

CHAPTER 2: GUIDED MEDITATION TO IMPROVE YOUR MOOD 24

CHAPTER 3: CLEAR YOUR MIND FOR PRODUCTIVITY | 5 MINUTES | 412 WORDS 55

CHAPTER 4: GUIDED MEDITATION AND MINDFULNESS ... 60

CHAPTER 5: HOW TO PREPARE FOR MEDITATION 63

CHAPTER 6: THE VALUE OF SLEEP 88

CHAPTER 7: THE STATE OF MEDITATION 100

CHAPTER 8: INDUCTION 109

CHAPTER 9: WHAT IS MEDITATION? 123

CHAPTER 10: A FULL GUIDE TO THE ART AND BENEFITS OF MEDITATION 138

CHAPTER 11: YOUR DIVINE SELF 153

CHAPTER 12: THE "CONSTANT CHANGE" MEDITATION . 165

Introduction

Before diving deeper into the different techniques, let me give you a few guidelines that will help you get the most out of your practice.

First of all, remember that to meditate you don't have to do anything special. Most people get confused on how to actually approach these techniques, because they believe they must "do something complicated", in order to reach a deep level of mental peace. In reality, just following my voice will be enough for you to dive deeper into your consciousness and relieve yourself from anxiety and stress.

Second of all, feel free to move during the practice if you are feeling uncomfortable. Trying to stay still in a position that does not allow you to relax will be detrimental to the meditation. Make any adjustment you deem necessary, moving will not affect your meditation session.

Finally, make sure to have at least 50 minutes to 1 hour of available time, as this is the rough time of each meditation in this book. If you are using your phone to listen to the meditations, I highly suggest you to download the book and put your phone in "do not disturb mode".

There is nothing more you need to know to have a great meditation and to get the most out of this book. Meditating is simple, do not complicate it.

Chapter 1: Why Meditate?

Figure 1: Free Credits

A Coherent Assessment

Mirror yourself this way, how have you progressed in life? What kind of life's resolutions do you usually take every time? And what about the remaining path of their life you have? Humankind has an aggregate of superior qualities and not so good ones. Can we say we have achieved the peak of our lives? Can we grow or can we remain as we are if that is not the case, then, how can we meet? Those questions as reality checks can make us come to the fact that positivity is specific and more so inevitable.

In our hectic modern life, we do a lot of myriads chores. From dust till dawn, our energy is sapped, the less power is left, and then we don't have more provisions to think about our causes of what makes us or brings us down. If we do any activity with good motives, we can gain more satisfaction. We have more things to relate and what we don't like may disappear. But the truth is that many of us continue to feel let down and frustrated by our contemporary lifestyle. Meditation aims to transform the mind. It does not have to be associated with any particular religion. Every one of us has a soul, and every one of us can work on it.

Is change desirable?

A minority of people would say they feel their lives are full of contentment. If they considered improving them, it would be to a limited extent. Others would also be sufficing to say that the little nuisances they can pinpoint to their lives are like ornaments to them so they become self-assured that this alchemy raises them from the within and they should feel comfortable to deal with it because that is their makeup, but they rarely know that this notion can lead them to miserable life's. Whereas a little meditation can make them better than those comfort zones, they feel satisfied.

If we can conceive how in scenario an individual can spend the whole day being subjected to a feeling of an ill-motive like jealousy, would this be a viable thing to do? Opposite of that if a suggestion would always be made to inundate your heart with goodies; all day long you would be more than willing to do that?

So matter what our social standing is, and our preferences are, our minds could tell that we are obsessed with predicaments. Our brains are inclined towards doubly our troubles, plagued with worries, furry, nursing the heartaches emanating from the unfair injustices of our friends. Encountering these instances, we can reason that, our feelings are manageable, and we can take our minds to the points of no turbulence of emotions. It sounds good. But the human being cannot control this. We can reason that is the way life is; we cannot control the happenings on our side, is natural, and most humans go through this. We can sit and reason that we don't have to act. It is it like having an ailment and assuming that it is natural to get a disease, and we don't need to consult the doctor. How wrong can that be?

Nobody wants afflictions or reason that if one could get sick all week long, that would be contrary to rational thoughts. Whatever our pursuits maybe such as walking and doing daily tasks, we have positive expectations emanating from the same. No one wants a life full of misery. If we expect life would always be abreast with agonies, we will not embark on any building initiatives. Other times we encounter thrilling mood boosters of activities, unbiased love from friends, calmness, positive confidence, but the feelings are temporary and fleeting. What if we can know how to steer our minds entirely to the wholesome experiences nonstop to our lives? Wonderfully our lives would be interwoven blissfully with happiness and excellent resonance.

A majority of people reason that life would be miserable, devoid suffering, and it would not make any sense. If humankind does not suffer inwardly, and we know what it feels like to go through hunger, wars, voracious greed, and hatred. The consequences are not worth it. We like the fact that the same life would be satisfying if people portray kindness and fulfillment. When we see others going through the positive aspects of life also ourselves, we also get uplifted.

Is change achievable?

Then the question remains, is change just a desire or a possibility? Some people think regardless of their circumstances; they cannot change without interfering with their inner selves.

The general rule is; one's life as far as the character is concerned does not change a lot. Verified research shows that if we could study a specific group of people after some years; we rarely can find morose people less miserable. Also, disorderly people may not be lesser disorganized. Those disturbed get oriented with goodness, while those who act with pretense learn to be humble. Changes can happen in both good and worst of all people. It signifies that reformation and change can happen no matter what the person is. The unusual thing is, those who are negative always have a hard time doing away with that trait. Those who agree they are inadequate, see the necessity to change. Nothing can work if we do not get the essence to work out our negative behaviors, and the same can persist for the worse for all our lives.

But those behavioral tendencies can be remedied and fixed. Wrath, corruption, ill feelings, are toxins in our bodies they are separable to us because we can dodge and brush them aside. For instance, think of water, a particular chemical can be mined and then became a poison. Also, the same water can be separated and became a healthy liquid to be used.

A Fundamental Aspect of Conscious Mess

Being aware of this involves our realization of that primary quality in itself. Consciousness comes merely by knowing. Similarly, with the water mentioned above with toxins, being aware is not but at day and night, the thoughts and emotions engulf us in our minds. Our consciousness is not affected because it is always present. Awareness makes us perceive what is good or not, and it permeates every emotion, sensation, reasoning's, hopes, and morbid fears as well.

Why Are Wishful Thoughts not enough?

We cannot be optional about how we appear now, but wishfully we can transform ourselves. We conjure those mental images; then our minds can have a sense of purpose and direction. But sitting there, wishing will not solve the hindrances at all costs. So acting should be on top of the list.

There is no problem anyone spending a countless hour learning a new art like writing, playing the guitar or any official skill. Remember we can also spend numerous hours in the gymnasium trying to reshape our body forms. What about expending ourselves tirelessly to free bikes that would not take a ride? What keeps us exerting ourselves to such things is nothing other than our thoughts and interests. This maximum interest is because we know there are paybacks in with time.

Mental work heeds some specific portfolios, but with little effort, can we achieve change? It is comparable to the process of learning the guitar. Can you achieve excellent results by sitting and wishing how you will one day play well? The positive outcome will result from doing it in the first instance.

We tend to expend a lot of determination to improve our lives facets, but the mental powers eventually are the ones which fathom our experiences. Meditation is one of the best ways of fixing our life or our wellbeing. Then if meticulously we discern the weakness we have on our hearts and mind and transform them into positivity, then that is automatically what we are talking about meditation.

What is meditation?

Meditation is a way of practicing to cultivate positivity of human traits as opposed to the bad. Any other form of practice would enact a person to become more proficient in an individual activity let say learning how to drive a car, play an instrument, and so forth. Globally we can find so many words that can mean 'meditation.'

Meditation aids everyone come into terms of understanding themselves and the world around them to foster qualities which can invigorate us unless we strive to weed them out.

So the startup could be like we can initiate the question within ourselves by asking what the purpose of this life is. Can someone be counted with the same kind of person he is? Can anyone improve himself self every time he wakes up? Those fundamental questions can build us up and help us see the need to improve ourselves.

We tend to think that shortcomings are part of us. We do not have anything we can resort to nothing else but to deal with them no matter sort of harm they have thrown at us. We cannot take that dysfunctionality forsake, knowing we can break out the vices of bad traits.

Every individual can get enlightened; even the Buddhist wisdom has portrayed that, from their ancient texts, every being has the potential for enlightenment. But the majority of humans are like impoverished beggars. They are affluent and poor but lack the insight that he is sitting on wealthy of gold treasures. Many individuals like that poor man do not have the know-how they can imbue themselves lives profound significance.

Transforming Young self- Change the world

Nurturing ourselves can be helpful to others; initially, our experiences can be a reference to some extent. What we don't want can be a prerequisite to avoid doing it to others. For instance, we can feel good when suffering, and on the same note, we will prevent at every margin to inflict others the same miseries of life. Because we need each other and everyone derives the best. So, we feel in the long run that happiness depends on what we do to ourselves and those around us. We know that self-centeredness is detrimental to us. It thrives if we have discontent on our lives. We may have superficial happiness, but if this does not reflect inside us, we do not experience the joy and compassion of others.

We don't think those ideals are high minded, but in reality, they throw the essence of the story back into the room.

Self-centered glee is making a name to oneself, or others, doomed. Other folks will think that to attain happiness is also theirs first, by isolating themselves from others and then foster theirs first. Without minding what others are feeling seeking happiness, selfishly is a sure way to make you, or anyone else feels doomed. That is total a misconception because none can be whole as a result of that and the results cannot worth telling. Because those who steer their boat towards this they find themselves in the coastlines of fear and hope. They can bring it to ruin the lives of those around them. What makes such assertions fake is that the earth we live in is not for some secluded personalities of those who conform to their kind of dress, beauty, and so forth. Everything was meant to depend on the other in a transformative manner. Coexistence is the only the way life becomes more bearable, and egos are not to be feed but to be curtailed at all means.

Unselfish love—also labeled as loving-kindness—is the tendency to wish for the others to truly attain the glee they deserve. Empathy is sympathizing with others and feeling what they are going through.

These are not void sentiments they are reality checks in our lives. Everyone out there wants to ease the misery of sufferings as possible. Because we interdepend on each other, our happiness or the lack of it is based on what we do to others, especially what we do to them.

Love and compassion are mighty friends in rare cases, do those who exhibit these qualities fail in their pursuits. Various researches show that those who love unconditionally and are compassionate to others can activate their brains for positive things. So eventual y such meditative attitude has an impact on us and those around as well.

What about the actions we do to others are to bear any fruits, they must be most of all, carrying the torch of wisdom. From the same knowledge, we get to be analytical and meditative. We can get more glimpses of what realty is, take us up, and in the long run, we make the world a better place to live in the grand scheme of things. If we transform ourselves, we better human beings and become doers of good not as masters over the other people. So meditation gives us noblest of all values we can think.

A Global Effect

Scientific evidence has portrayed that, you don't have to be an expert in meditation so that you can attain the full benefits. Fifteen minutemen every day can make a lot of changes in your life reduction of stress, being one of them individually in these modern times we are living. Anxiety can also get curtailed, avert the effects of depression in life. Surgical procedures have also get linked to early deaths, but after meditation immune system improves significantly.

To what intensity can we discipline our mind to work constructively—for example, by replacing obsession with contentment, agitation with calmness, or hatred with kindness? Twenty years ago, it was almost universally accepted by neuroscientists that the brain contained all its neurons at birth. The concept was that their number did not change in adult life. We now know that new neurons get produced up until the moment of death. Scientists speak of "neuroplasticity," which is the brain's ability to change its structure and function continually. It happens in response to new experiences, so that appropriate training, such as learning a musical instrument or a sport, can bring significant and lasting functional and structural changes in the brain. Mindfulness, altruism, and other necessary human qualities can get cultivated in the same way. In general, if we repeatedly engage in a new activity or train in a new skill, modifications in the neuronal system of the brain can be observed within a month. It is essential, therefore, to meditate regularly.

Studies on the brain working have astounded the scientific world. It got considered as a strange idea to that, but now, a new lease of life has been given to the mainstream research fields of science. Let us think of magnetic resonance imaging, very complicated indeed, but neuroscience comprehension has been achieved primarily in this advanced technological age of ours. Everything has not got discovered, but, we have at least seen much of the contemplative inner powers of the mind.

A life of satisfaction can come from grappling with the challenges of our existence, not just free-flowing experience without much ado and unpleasant sensations. Mind training makes it better for us to deal with mental poisons like biases, hate, self-centeredness, and irrational fears, and more the right perception of the realities within ourselves. Eventually, we can tap out resources to grapple with the retreats of life devoid of distractions and more so we draw intense exercise from them at last.

The problem for many people in life is that they underrate the capacity to bring some changes to life. Our characters loopholes remain the same as long as we lower the bar for us to bring dramatic changes to us.

What we might refer to a normal to us, it could still be where the starting point should be and not the goal to get aimed. We should know that life is more worthwhile; some drastic practical steps will eventually take us into our destination.

Measurements regarding how meditation and mind training can impact our lives cannot entirely get told. Experiences can get turned for the better and inward revolution can happen profoundly in peace

Source of Inspiration

Unfortunately, the majority of people have a deep-seated mindset that they were born this way. They cannot change that, unconsciously that conviction of wrong notions is not good because it makes us not to rise above our weak points. Many people can say they have experienced this feeling during their prime age. It can haunt others even when they are in the workplace. If the victims of this cannot alter that wrong thinking that means every attempt is just another faltering in life.

Sometimes you try to talk to people, and one of the changes they would like to have is through their convictions and confirmations. If nothing seems to bear fruits, they usually call it off. When their opinions and prayer don't work, they dismiss the notion of working with the mindset as the novice designated to make decisions. But scientists have unanimously agreed that the brain can be steered to achieve positive results.

Chapter 2: Guided Meditation To Improve Your Mood

Awful mindsets appear to make no sense. It's normal to witness the calmest and gathered individual go from upbeat and tranquil to nervous and tense inside only a couple of minutes. While anxiety can be a major piece of the human condition, nobody can be impeccably cheerful and constructive constantly. Plus, without having any strength over these emotional episodes, an individual, as well as job relations, can turn out to be increasingly stressed.

In any case, it is hard to put the finger on the main driver of an awful mind-set. While nosey neighbors, slow drivers, discourteous partners, and cold espresso can trigger a reaction that is negative although the fundamental causes probably will not be so quick. When it comes to a way of life, having feelings like intemperate negative reasoning, poor sleep habits, and even the customary ingestion of stimulants and intoxicants can likewise add to anxiety and mental pressure.

When feeling tense and uneasy, it is a lot simpler to give as little chance to start an awful state of mind. In the event that this circumstance sounds recognizable to you, think about attempting meditation, one of the most straightforward and quickest approaches to set yourself up for a superior day.

How Your Mood Benefits From Meditation

When managing repeating episodes of touchiness and temper issues, it does nothing more than trouble as you try to overlook the issue. In many cases, the genuine reason for a bad-tempered character or negative sentiments is little and effectively settled once distinguished.

With regards to building the sort of mindfulness and self-esteem that can smooth out those wrinkles in mental uneasiness, nothing beats meditation.

In the event that you are not totally acquainted with the ideas of care and meditation, the following are the key advantages of meditation to improve your state of mind.

Perceive Terrible Temperaments

Meditation contemplates extended care, making the likelihood to perceive a dreadful perspective as it begins and keeping an eye on it rather than empowering it to put a damper on your day.

Achieve a Superior Comprehension of Your Feelings

Care obviously includes how transient a dreadful attitude really is. Throughout meditation, you regain the care of self and are able to get rid of all awful thoughts of the mind and allowing you to gain acknowledgment.

Awful demeanors can be connected with reasons of fault or other negative emotions, which just breeds an all the more terrible attitude. Meditation is connected to watching estimations and insights without judgment or commitment. Through affirmation of the way in which you feel, it is more straightforward to deal softly and discreetly with yourself and individuals around you.

Figure out how to Adore Yourself

Setting aside an effort to become acquainted with yourself better and taking into account your basic needs requires internal quality and expanded self-esteem. These characteristics assemble mental and enthusiastic strength and an equal state of mind.

Picking the Correct Fundamental Oils for Controlling moods and Supporting Meditation

The development of care through meditation can help to realize valuable changes in the manner in which you can obviously handle mental stressors, a passionate miracle can make it hard to discover the harmony, tranquility, and solace expected to start a profitable procedure toward more prominent care. You will be glad to realize that this has been looked at previously, and arrangements have been proposed.

Aromatics, for instance, have been utilized closely during the act of meditation for quite a long time. This is nothing unplanned either—the amazing natural mixes discharged from incense and fundamental oils can ground the brain and loosen up the body, making the ideal climate for meditation. Matching fundamental oils to your particular awful state of mind can permit not just the improvement of the nature of your meditation session, but it can also lift a portion of the sentiments of an awful mindset to set them free.

Angry, Frustrated, Impatient, or Annoyed

At the point when emotions flare and persistence runs low, the psyche goes into overdrive considering complex arrangements, forceful plans, and cautious reactions. This can make the mind uneasy and powers mindfulness in a multidirectional strain.

This is why you must be able to Balance outrage with the sort of clearness and mental discharge that originates from remaining in a clear mental state.

Upset or Melancholy

When feeling lower than the base of a well, the general concept of pausing for a minute alone with the brain can appear to be welcome for a surge of pessimism.

Prior to attempting to accumulate mindfulness, consider crushing through the pessimism with some sweet-smelling tokens of what an extraordinary individual you are.

Excited and Giddy

Surely, even constructive emotions can give indications of the progress of individuals every so often. A happy character going around in impressive personalities can be hard to tame. When imagining a noteworthy event, wearing down an endeavor that gets the innovative personality, or essentially feeling especially happy to be animated, the cerebrum can end up being genuinely powerful.

In spite of the way that there is nothing awry with being especially happy, repressing the empowered character is critical for keeping up mental equality similarly as the focus during meditation.

Stressed or Anxious

Stress and anxiety are not only a badly designed truth about current society or an inhibitor to smooth meditation. An ever-increasing number of studies have featured the negative physical and psychological wellness results of the abundance of anxiety. Creating a vulnerable individual and making them fall apart due to an assortment of physical and mental situations.

Exhausted or Mentally Fatigued

Although an individual can seem troubled, it is without a doubt a lot easier if their brain remains focused and sharp. Following a long workweek or especially tiring day, the mind can feel about as red hot as a piece of coal and seriously requiring a blaze of life to take care.

Mental exhaustion can happen to everyone, displaying as a detectable move in enthusiastic states. This is a trademark bit of life, and the sentiments ought to be different depending upon a wide variety of conditions. You can plan to feel through and through various when getting a charge out of a brilliant night on the town with a friend than you would after the sixth hour of working through a rough day at work.

Little and even tremendous mental exhaustion can be a key bit of a standard day by day where the presence can be achieved by a wide combination of components. For example, body rhythms expect a gigantic activity in the way individuals feel at different events of the day and even different events of the year.

During the early night, a person's critical levels can be high and the assumptions can be euphoric and red hot. Before long, when the sun goes down and the day's exertion has negatively impacted the body, feelings can drop to a lower amount, which can be experienced as gradualness.

The critical thing to comprehend is that there is nothing out of request with encountering these enthusiastic advancements, and a bit of the time will not make them leave. Regardless, without proper, solid techniques for overseeing stress for countering these fiery advancements, they can start to antagonistically impact the body.

Finding a Solution

While there is no requirement for worry about changes in feelings, the way to keeping mood swings inside good levels is through understanding and mindfulness. In the event that moodiness has proceeded for drawn-out timeframes and is presently influencing work and connections, setting aside the effort to consider an answer is significant for mental dependability and long haul joy and prosperity.

On the off chance that the anxiety levels are serious, counseling with a human services person or therapist is best for setting up a routine that works for you. Nevertheless, this routine can be enhanced with a portion of the procedures featured beneath for expanded adequacy.

Track Emotional Patterns

The most ideal approach to figure out the main reason for the occurrences is by maintaining a record of every occurrence. Taking notes of significant changes allow you to establish a relationship with different elements that could be the influencer of your anxiety.

Exercise More

Never doubt the considerable therapeutic power of regular exercise. There is nothing that takes control over the mind and body and the most ideal approach to figure out the reason for your high anxiety than by enjoying a rigorous exercise routine.

Improve Sleeping Patterns

The estimation of rest and legitimate advancement through all rest cycles is basic for keeping up with the adjustments in the body. The decreased quality of rest can be influenced by any unnatural light sources, stress, and many other different conditions. This can cause an individual to portray bitterness and bad moods, which can ultimately cause unnecessary anxiety.

Improve Nutrition

The sustenance that you eat is in like manner a great drug that helps keep you happy, sound, and relaxed during an evening out. At the same time, you should think about decreasing any and all alcohol, caffeine, and sugar in order to maintain a healthy and balanced body.

How Examination Controls Mood

It is clear that examining frameworks that specialists suggest for controlling negative emotions can help with the adjustment. When utilized the individual can expect an immediate effect in the way the mood swings affect them.

In light of this, another development has unimaginable implications in the way of adjustment and care. This is found through mindfulness, as it is the moment-to-moment awareness of the sensations, processes, and thoughts within and outside of the body.

As indicated by the Harvard Help Guide, contemplation is tied in with taking a target point of view on the negative portrayals in the brain and building up a condition of quiet and calm. This enables the psyche to communicate to the body concerning the control of all negative feelings.

Through care or reflection, it is conceivable to develop more clear mindfulness and point of view through watching the brain in its characteristic easy state unaffected by outside components. Truth be told, an examination distributed in Wildernesses in Human Neuroscience distributed a broad investigation on how reflection and care can be a successful device for adjusting and a better understanding of the feelings.

Subjects were provided with an 18-minute introduction to learning a new language. Furthermore, specialists at Michigan State University (MSU) have discovered proof to help this contention. They have discovered that rehearsing care helps the psychological capacity for all people, not simply the individuals who practice it consistently.

The investigation they performed was intended to find whether care was a condition that must be accomplished by a professional, or on the off chance that any individual who needs to center their brain could do it as well.

The analysts chose a gathering of 68 ladies who had never attempted any type of care of well-being. Moreover, a logically approved study of the female subjects demonstrated that none of them had a particular limit or tendency to the care.

The subjects were then isolated into two gatherings, one of which took an interest in an 18-minute guided meditation that acquainted them with the ideas of care and the other group with nothing.

After this arrangement, the two gatherings were given some predetermined negative visual upgrades and their enthusiastic reactions were recorded. This piece of the test included pictures portraying antagonistic feelings, military clashes, and even some grim and realistic pictures intended to sincerely inconvenience the psyche.

The outcomes demonstrated that the ladies who reflected had the option to show passionate guideline ordinarily found in the individuals who practice care consistently. This was obvious through observing mind action that showed resilience to the emotional shock factor and kept emotional responses in check.

The examination presumed that a few people have an attitude of familiarity with the present condition. The individuals, who are not, nevertheless, can pick up the advantages of this perspective through rehearsing reflection.

Besides, care and contemplation are especially similar to the quality and best developed through exercise after some time as opposed to flexed and connected at the time of extraordinary need. Indeed, even a 20-minute care practice every day is sufficient to start picking up these advantages.

Notwithstanding the more straightforward impacts of contemplation on enthusiastic equalization, care has appeared to change the capacity of the brain. This enables it to be increasingly indisposed to a positive and sympathetic point of view, taking the care of incredible expansion to everyday practice for building up more noteworthy enthusiastic interactions.

Practical Guide to Meditation for Mood Swings

The standards and routine with regards to care and reflection have picked up a devoted following of specialists who swear by its advantages to physical and psychological wellness.

The main necessity for rehearsing such care is a working personality. From that point, advancement will go to the extent that the responsibility to practice can proceed.

The act of care develops an enthusiastic separation that enables space to reflect between the fundamental self and individual responses to the earth and inward conditions. A definitive objective is to develop care that would then be able to be connected to each snapshot of the day.

The key strides to starting reflection for directing mood swings are featured beneath.

Set a Time

You need not bother with a pagoda by the lake or anything over the tranquility and quiet of a peaceful corner of your reality unable to rehearse meditation. In any case, you should commit some time to the opportunity for this training and guarantee you will not put it off.

Developing Care

It is anything but difficult to confound meditation by stopping the brain, hushing the psyche, or applying authority over the psyche. In any case, the thought is to focus on the minute without decisions as opposed to controlling the occasion.

Managing Diversions

The inwardly pained personality will not generally sit still and remain centered and this can offer an increased amount of decisions and more noteworthy disorder. Try not to battle this or attempt to stop this. Basically watch the musings as they go through the psyche, both positive and negative. Be thankful for such a proficient personality, that keeps you mindful of your worries and return your concentration to watching the present moments.

This is the place the instinctive methodology becomes possibly the most important factor. Those new to care and contemplation might be astounded by how the brain carries on, where it goes, and how precarious it very well may be to settle down and center around the occasion.

Never judge your psyche or yourself for any of this, as this would be counterproductive. Rather, practice the significant quality of coming back to the point of view of an onlooker, and in time, you will ace meditation.

Guided Meditation for Mood Exercises and Scripts

Consider something in your life you are amazingly grateful for, think about where you can feel that in your body. Think of standing out enough to notice the things in your life that you are thankful for.

Basically, enable gratefulness to come up regularly. Also, when it comes up just let yourself sink into the tendency by being ready. Notice how it feels in your body, how your imperativeness feels. Likewise, if it does not come up that is okay; you do not need to endeavor to make yourself feel it. Essentially offer up to your heart, not your head.

So let us streak through all pieces of your life that you might be appreciative for.

Immediately convey your thoughtfulness regarding your breath, as you take in and as you release a breath out and the manner, in which that all of these breaths gives your life.

By then, think about your heart pounding, thumping, stacking up with fondness and compassion and concordance, and spilling that feeling.

Convey your thoughtfulness regarding your eyes that let you see faces, smiles, nature, the daybreak, the sunset, the rainbow, the moon, and the stars, and yourself in the mirror.

Carry your attention to your ears, which allow sound, music, giggling, and the voices of those you cherish as well as the quietness and lovely hints of life.

Carry your attention to your nose that scents the sea breeze, the fragrance of sweet aroma, the blooms, the trees, recently cut grass, and the drifting scents that originate from the kitchen, cupcakes in the stove.

Carry your attention to your lips and mouth that smile and enjoys and supports, kisses and talks and murmurs, and sings.

Carry your attention to your hands that touch and hold, and stroke, and open and close, and clap, and crush, the arms, and shoulders that convey, embrace, lift, and stretch.

Our feet, our toes, the blessing to squirm them, transport you, walk, run, dangle, move, kick, overlap, jump, and point.

Shouldn't something be said about your tears, your distresses, in the quality that you appear to have the option to marshal, to endure every day?

Carry your attention to your wealth, your development, your advancement, your point of view moves, the fortune and stream and sympathy and love and light, and your capacity to see development, and potential in each minute.

Presently simply inhale and feel more elegance, and simplicity.

What's more, presently experience the glow, love, and sympathy that appreciation brings into your heart.

Float your attention to sustaining connections throughout your life, the new ones, and the more seasoned ones.

Material things that came to you surprisingly, things that stream to you with extraordinary exertion and duty, diligent work.

Consider love in your life, and your association with those things that are sweet, and cherishing and fair, and simply feel right.

When we never again underestimate life, we become thankful for everything that we have.

Simply inhale and feel this stream.

Gratitude Meditation

As you start this meditation for mindfulness, begin by using something that you are currently experiencing. It could be something in nature like the swaying of a tree, or the warmth that you feel on your skin from the sun, or perhaps you feel many comforts as you sit in a chair or just taking a break from it all to sit and pause for a moment. No matter what it is, choose one so you can allow it and notice it inside of your experience.

Give appreciation and gratitude a chance to emerge and fill your body and psyche.

Presently consider somebody you do not know well yet who has bolstered your experience today in one way or another. It could be a transport driver, the individual who stacked the organic product in the supermarket, or the writer of the book that you are currently reading.

Enable yourself to feel how you have profited by the work that you do. Enable yourself to feel appreciation and gratitude. Consider the apparatuses that you utilize that help your work and your life. You are the PC, your books, structures, hardware. Pick a certain something and consider every one of them is required for its creation. Acknowledge and feel gratitude that you approach these instruments. Feel gratitude for individuals you work and live with.

Think about a specific individual whose work or exertion legitimately underpins your work throughout everyday life. Value their commitment, their honest goal, saying in your brain to them, "Much obliged."

Presently infer somebody you care about. Picture them in your head.

As you envision them, see what sentiments you are encountering, what sensations you identify in your body, particularly those that surround your heart.

Give yourself a chance to offer thanks to them. Expressing gratitude toward them for being their identity and for their quality in your life. Envision them getting your gratitude.

Presently infer something, specifically, you are thankful for now. Feel the appreciation and gratitude for its essence in your life.

As you convey these things in your mind for what you are grateful for, empower yourself to rest in the experience.

When you develop the act of gratitude, you may even get yourself ready to be appreciative for troublesome or terrible encounters.

In the event that you would like to infer an involvement in your life that is testing, one for which you would like to have the option to offer thanks.

Offer your gratitude and appreciation. Thank this test for what it might offer you. Gratitude for our body, gratitude for our psyche, gratitude for the straightforward reality of being alive right now.

Finally, value the chance to delay and experience this very routine with regards to gratitude in itself. For all that, you have inferred during this meditation, for the majority of the incalculable blessings throughout your life, state, "Much obliged."

To every one of the individuals, to all that is around you, and part of you. For all that, you have encountered in your life, for the majority of this, much obliged.

Enable the feeling of gratitude to fill you totally, as you take in and breathe out.

Choosing the breath directly here, at the present time, completely alive and present in this exact instant.

Completion with a full breath in and a long moderate breathe out. Delicately and gradually, open your eyes and return your attention to where you are.

In case you would like to grow the demonstration of gratitude meditation, build up the inclination for thinking of something you feel thankful for every morning right when you wake up. In case it empowers, feel obliged to record it in a journal. You may similarly try conveying appreciation today to a person for whom you feel grateful.

Chapter 3: Clear Your Mind For Productivity | 5 Minutes | 412 Words

Hello and thank you for joining me in this meditation to clear your mind for productivity. Like computers, it is so important to take the time to clear your mind. If a computer gets too cluttered with files, data and applications it gets slow and frustrating to work with. The mind is very similar. Too many thoughts can clog up our own computing power and can make things slow and frustrating to work with. We need to take the time to love our own minds as much as we take the time to love other parts of our lives. Our minds organize, interpret, and structure our lives- A calm mind allows us to be in harmony with our surroundings and to feel at peace with what is going on.

To begin, take some time to settle into your chair.

Feeling your body resting on the chair.

Feeling your lower legs and buttocks pressed against the chair.

Feeling your feet on the ground.

Feeling your back pressed up against the back of the chair.

Feeling the gentle sensations of gravity pulling you towards the Earth.

Pulling your awareness from your mind into the sensations of your body.

Breathing in and out from the bottom of your belly.

Imagine that all the thoughts in your mind could just melt out of your head into the Earth beneath you.

Feel it pouring out of your awareness, away from your body, and away from your experience.

All of your necessary thoughts, background noise, inner critic thoughts, and anything else you wish to release for your mind, letting it fall down into the ground.

Letting it fall away from your awareness.

Dripping away from your mind effortlessly, and forever.

Breathing in clarity, and breathing out clutter.

Releasing what you do not need.

Feeling the Earth absorbing these thoughts forever.

Letting everything go even more.

Deepening your breath.

Coming back into the sensations of your feet.

Coming back into the sensations of your legs.

Coming back into the sensations of your torso.

Coming back into the sensations of your arms.

Coming back into the sensations of your hands.

Coming back into the sensations of your neck.

Coming back into the sensations of your head.

As you move back into your life, see if you can release your thoughts during the day. Anytime something worrisome or bothersome comes up, just let it all go.

Thank you for listening to this meditation. Have a wonderful day full of mental clarity.

Chapter 4: Guided Meditation And Mindfulness

Mindfulness is about observation without criticism, being kind and compassionate with yourself. When stress or unhappiness hover overhead, rather than taking it all personally, you learn to treat them as if they were black clouds in the sky and you learn to observe them with curiosity as they float by.

Guided Meditation is simply meditation with the help of a guide. It is one of the easiest ways to enter into a state of deep relaxation and inner stillness. It is one of the most powerful ways to eliminate stress and bring about positive personal changes within yourself.

As the brain does not distinguish between an imagined event and a real one, the experience you have with a guided meditation is just like having a real experience. This has an amazing effect on your life due to the way the brain works.

While you are in this deeply relaxed state of mind, your subconscious is open to positive suggestions, and your guide will use this time to take you on an inner journey that is designed to improve one or more aspects of your life.

I am hoping that reading my Guided Meditations you will benefit from imagining you are doing something else or you are somewhere else.

It enables you to switch off from your anxieties and problems for a few mins and helps you to calm down and relax.

The brain will quite often come back to your problems but this is quite normal and what the brain does. You can very gently bring your attention back to the guided imagery meditation.

Less than 10 minutes of hypnotic guided meditation can reduce stress and blood pressure.

I hope you enjoy these short and pleasant guided meditations and you can read them any time during the day or night.

Chapter 5: How To Prepare For Meditation

While meditation can be undertaken just about anywhere at just about any given time, there are certain guidelines that you need to follow if you want your meditation to be as effective as possible. However, keep in mind that meditation is meant to be flexible. The idea is not to create a rigid system that you will find difficult to follow. Meditation is meant to be easy and modifiable to adjust it to meet your specific needs.

Seating and Posture

We will start by discussing the five basic meditative postures. Your job is to identify which posture works for you in most situations and try to stick to it. While certain meditative practices do require you to follow a specific meditative posture, most of them can be adapted to alternative postures as well.

Chair Meditation

Because most of us tend to work 9-to-5 jobs, realistically speaking we do tend to spend most of our time seated in an office chair of some sort. Chair meditation is a great way to break your midday monotony without ever having to leave your station. For seated meditation, you're going to want to straighten your back and ensure that you are touching the floor with your feet. Ideally your knees should be bent at a 90-degree angle, and your back should be as straight as possible. If you're not sure what you want to do with your hands, try simply resting them on your knees.

Standing Meditation

Sometimes you want to get out of your chair, and may be more comfortable trying a standing method. You're going to want to start by standing so that your feet are at your shoulder length apart. Bend your knees slightly, and allow pressure of your entire day to ease out through your body all the way down to your feet. As you do so adjust your hands so they are placed gently across your stomach, so that you can feel every breath that moves through your body as you embark on your personal mission.

Cross-legged Meditation

Another posture you can explore if you feel comfortable, is the traditional Indian cross-legged sitting posture. This particular posture is actually the most commonly recommended posture from meditative activities, The idea is to keep your legs crossed under each other, with your hips elevated slightly higher than the heels of your feet. If you are new to meditation, it is generally recommended that you try this posture with a cushion or a towel or some sort of soft surface underneath you so that you don't hurt yourself, since it can be difficult to hold if you are not used to it. If you feel there's too much pressure on your heels, try bringing one of your legs across the other so that the ankle of one is positioned on top of the knee of the other leg. You could alternatively bring full heels across the thighs of the opposite leg in what is commonly known as the Lotus position.

The Burmese position is slightly different in that you don't cross your legs. Instead, you can position your feet so the ankles of each foot are bent inward and facing towards the pubic area – this posture is generally preferred by those individuals who find it difficult to cross their legs.

Kneeling Meditation

If you want to keep your spine straight but don't feel comfortable crossing your legs, another great alternative is to kneel. Traditionally, this is known as the Virasana or the Vajrasana. Here you start by bending your knees and resting your body weight along the length of your shins. Your ankles should be tucked under your bottom. For ease and comfort you can opt to insert a rolled yoga mattress or a tube of some sort between your bottom and your knees.

This particular position is customarily easier than the cross-legged position, and is also generally pain-free, so your ankles will thank you.

Horizontal Meditation

If however none of these positions suit you, or you are trying a sleep inducing meditation, you will find that the posture of choice is generally the horizontal posture. As you lay down, be careful to ensure that your feet are parted at shoulder length, similar to the standing meditation posture, and your arms are laying at your sides instead of folded across your body. If you find this posture uncomfortable, you can bend your knees and elevate your hips slightly to help adjust yourself.

Attuning to Physical Sensations

The physical world around you impacts your mind. This is a fact that we are all aware. What we don't necessarily notice is that just as the physical world impacts our mind, our mind in turn, also impacts our physical form. In the world of meditation this form of comprehensive understanding is referred to as body sensing.

Think of the last time you were happy. In addition to feeling mentally excited, how did you feel on a physical level? Were you in pain? Did you find it difficult to move? Or did you feel uneasy for some reason?

Odds are you didn't feel any of this – why? When you are happy and relaxed, you don't feel physically unwell. In fact you tend to feel lighter and more physically relaxed. At the same time, the exact opposite happens when you are dealing with some sort of emotional upset. You might feel nauseous or uneasy when you're freaking out before a major exam, for example. Or, maybe you tend to feel lethargic when you are depressed or dealing with huge amounts of mental stress. Your body is a reflection of your mind. If you feel happy, your body is also happier and you are more at peace. Whereas, when you are distressed, your physical form tends to manifest in a way that reflects that negativity.

As you prepare yourself to practice meditation, one of the things you are going to want to ensure is that you are working on your ability to understand what your body is saying to you. The easiest way to do this is by practicing body sensing. Body sensing not only allows you to control your central nervous system and allow your mind to achieve a deeper form of mental and physical relaxation, it is also known to boost your body's natural resilience. This work will help develop your ability to experience a more solid and constant sense of wholeness and well-being, in a manner unattached to your external obstacles.

Emotional Focus

As you prepare to embark on your meditative journey, another factor that you are going to need to look into is Emotional self focus. One of the core objectives of meditation is to promote self-care. In fact, meditation itself is known to have extremely therapeutic properties. Emotion focused therapy is actually a short-term psychotherapy approach that is commonly included in most meditative guides. The logic applied here is simple - emotion focused meditations are meant to identify, and cull the innate emotions the participant has. This form of the elimination of a specific emotion may be problematic to a person's growth and development, since eliminating a specific emotion in its entirety can cause people to develop mental blocks.

Research has shown that emotion focused therapy helped participants identify with their own self, which in turn allowed them to better manage their emotional experiences. Mental health issues such as depression, complex trauma etc. have shown improvement when associated with emotion focused meditations, which is why it has been used specifically to help individuals with the internalized stigma of sexual orientation, for example

As you practice using the provided meditative guides, it is important that you focus on trying to attain a specific goal during the meditative process. This ensures that you are focusing on self-care and self-awareness. As you grow up you will find that it is much easier to focus on the needs of other people rather than those of your own. However, even though this is commonplace, simply put it is not right. Remembering your own needs and feelings is just as important as tending to those of others. Furthermore, it is equally important that you ensure that your self-sacrificing mindset doesn't lead to you suppressing your own emotional needs and depriving yourself of the help that you require.

Meditation can only help you once you have begun to consciously focus on your own wants and needs. Keep in mind that the goal you set for yourself is an important part of your personal meditation. By using your meditative goals and manifesting empathy, you have the ability to attune yourself to the needs of others. But this ability can only truly manifest when you have come to terms with your own needs and have accepted yourself for who you are. Once you start to take care of yourself better you'll be better equipped to take care of others as well.

You deserve to be happy, and are a good person. These are the thoughts that you need to live by.

Identifying and Dealing with Bodily Pain

Another important factor to prepare for a meditative lifestyle, is clarity in terms of what you are working towards. Let's say for instance you are working toward dealing with physical pain. You are going to need to know specifically what kind of pain you are trying to deal with. Understanding the basis and depth of your pain will help you choose which meditative guides are going to be most effective for you.

When it comes to dealing with bodily pain, it is important that you make it a point to understand which pain management technique would be best suited for your ailment. Body-scanning allows an individual to mentally "x-ray" their body, identify their points of pain and then address or heal them as they go.

Another important form of pain management meditation is the mindful-movement technique. This technique teaches individuals to use mindful-movements, such as standing in a specific posture and then proceeding to go through a list physical actions, including rotating your hands and shoulders, stretching your arms, and breathing in and out at specific intervals. This type of focused breathing is another common pain management technique that can assist individuals with relaxation issues and chronic pain.

Physical Distractions

In addition to all of this, there are also a multitude of issues that you are going to want to avoid if you wish your meditation to go smoothly. For starters you're going to want to ensure that you have the proper set-up. This starts with the space where you have chosen to practice your meditation. Other factors to consider include the surrounding ambient noise, or your viewpoint from that physical space. So, always try to ensure that you have chosen a calm, empty space where you can minimize interruptions and allow yourself to relax. If you can, try to get some time outside, or at least make sure your space is well ventilated so that you have fresh air before or while you are meditating. The more fresh air you let in, the easier you will find it is to project yourself outside of the four walls you are constantly crammed in.

Begin this process by detaching yourself from any external stimuli. Turn off your phone before you embark on your meditative session. Although it is understandable that detaching yourself from social media or your phone can be difficult, particularly if you are a parent, putting in the extra effort to ensure that your children are in a safe place while you take 30 minutes for yourself is well worth it. In fact, that in itself is one of the reasons why early mornings are often considered to be an ideal time to meditate. Not only is it more than likely that you will be free of any external commitments, it is also generally a quieter time of the day.

Soft tranquil beats and musical rhythms, such as ambient music or simple instrumental tracks work well for creating a relaxing space. There are also meditative tracks and music selections available online at popular streaming sites. These are specifically composed to help add an additional level to your meditative depth.

Building Focal Points

Another extremely important part of the meditative process is finding your mind's true intent. Generally, meditation practices ask you to set an intention prior to beginning any session. This allows you to fully appreciate and utilize your meditative time. You can pre-program your meditative focus or intent by using a mental questionnaire process. Start by asking simple questions, like 'Why am I meditating?', 'What do I hope to gain from meditating?', 'What is my purpose?', 'Who am I?', 'What do I want to be?', 'How do I get where I want to be?' etc.

The idea here is to use the question to center yourself before you start meditating, so that your meditation focuses on that specific point. This is similar to how compasses show you true north, with a magnet constantly bringing the arrow back to it. Keep in mind that meditation does not have to be religious. Although certain people meditate in order to experience God, and to build on that consciousness, belief in a higher power does not increase your ability to meditate.

Meditation can also be about you finding the proper wavelength for your thoughts and experiences. Is important to keep in mind, however, that although focused meditative instruction may seem superfluous, your meditative energy depends on the mind-set that you begin the meditative guide with. Taking time out to focus on your intention will not only help increase the efficiency of your meditative guide it will also help you maximize on this time you are taking for yourself.

Meditative Breathing Techniques

While there are multiple meditative breathing processes and practicing, for the purposes of this brief guide, we will be concentrating on five specific techniques that allow you to better induce meditative focus; they are Shamantha, Nadi

Shondhana, Zuanqi, Khumbaka Pranayama and Box Breathing.

Shamantha is a Buddhist breathing technique that teaches you to breathe in your natural rhythm. Generally, Shamantha breathing is known as the "reset breathing" technique, because it is meant to help you come back to the present moment. In order to practice Shamantha breathing you need to first relax your body, and stretch out your spine. As you do, you are trying to find a still spot to focus your attention – that point is your focus, and it is where all your breath travels to and where it comes back from. As you focus your breathing you start to allow the natural rhythm of your breathing to course through your body, and like a rudderless boat in open seas, you simply relax and allow yourself to ride each breath as it travels through your entire body, and back out. Focus only on your breathing. Even as you wander off to different thoughts, your breathing continues to bring you back like an anchor. Shamantha breathing has been shown to help deter age-based cognitive decline, and as such is one of the best breathing techniques to use while practicing meditation.

The next form of meditative breathing that is favored by practitioners is the Nadi Shondhana technique. This type of breathing is used as a purifying technique that originates from Hinduism. This meditative practice allows your body to find its inner balance by using controlled source breathing. Nadi Shondhana is known more widely as Alternate Nostril Breathing, where each side of the nostril is blocked while the other is used to breathe for a certain period of time to assist in the smooth flow of airflow. Each side is blocked for about thirty seconds to a minute each, and the body is taught to breathe through just one nostril at a time. The exercise generally lasts for about fifteen to twenty minutes, and doing so can help reduce high levels of blood pressure and help improve reactiveness. The breathing technique is particularly well known for allowing both hemispheres of the brain to get a physical and mental workout and can help with activities that require left and right motor senses to align.

Zhuanqi originates from Taoism and is a soft breathing technique that helps the body to harmonize with nature and their surroundings. The objective of Zhuanqi is simple. By uniting your breath in mind you continue to breathe in and out, until your breathing has reached a gentle consistency. For beginners, the trick to understanding whether or not you are properly practising Zhuanqi is to notice when your breathing has gone absolutely quiet. Start by finding yourself a comfortable position, straighten your back and close your eyes, and as you do mentally focus your view on the tip of your nose. Carefully breathe in and out through your abdomen until you can hear your breathing start to quiet down. Your abdomen should be moving deeply outward with each breath that is drawn and inward as you expel the breath. As you do so, try to keep your diaphragm as still as possible, and repeat.

Khumbhaka Pranayamas, better known as the Antara and Bahya are two Hinduism inspired breathing techniques melded together to form what we refer to as intermittent breathing. The Khumbhaka Pranayamas are best practiced in an upright sitting position or alternatively in a standing posture. Prostate positions, or laying down are not advisable due to the nature of the exercise. To begin, expel all of the existing air in your lungs and then proceed to carefully inhale with your mouth until your lungs are once again full. In between breaths, once the air has been drawn in, hold the air in your lungs and after a brief pause begin to slowly release the breath. After emptying out your lungs, instead of automatically drawing in your next breath abstain for about 3 to 4 seconds. This is known as Bahya; this short deprivation will allow you to breathe in deeper and hold your breath longer, as the cycle repeats.

The Box Breathing technique uses a combination of slow breaths, and is predominantly practiced to relieve stress or anxiety. Unlike the other meditative breathing techniques mentioned here, Box Breathing, also commonly known as four-square breathing, can help regulate multiple pulmonary diseases including

COPD or chronic obstructive pulmonary disease, and asthma. Similar to the Khumbhaka Pranayamas, you begin the process by expelling the excess air from your lungs and drawing in fresh air. However as you draw in air, you breath to a slow count of four. You then hold your breath for four seconds, and then finally release the breath to the count of four before repeating the process.

3 Levels of Meditative Knowledge

Another factor to be aware of as you embark on your meditative journey is how meditation leads to different levels of consciousness. Generally, meditation can lead to three specific levels; subconscious, consciousness, and super-consciousness.

Your sub-consciousness begins as a dulled form of awareness, where you can sense but not necessarily pinpoint the direct result of the experiences you have had.

This level of your mind is like the secondary market in economics. There is a constant flow of goods or in this case experiences, and there are no rigid constraints to tie them down, which is why the awareness is so faint. This part of your consciousness can, however, cross over to your consciousness at times, which is where rationality and logic begin to govern the wayward thoughts that you are projecting in such a manner that that you have a more clear and organized thought process.

The consciousness is the file cabinet of your mind. Here you are meant to sort out your thoughts and organize them in such a way that you can find and access them with ease, when needed. You may also begin to notice that, at the consciousness level, the thoughts and opinions of other people start to play a significant role in how you perceive or react to things.

The superconscious is the problem-solving part of your consciousness. Here, all information is filtered in terms of relevance and then used to draw a specific conclusion. Your decisions, for example, are meant to be a natural reaction to your abilities and the problem at hand. This is why the superconscious is known for the mental clarity that emerges, that then allows you to make better, more informed decisions.

Chapter 6: The Value Of Sleep

A decent night's rest is extraordinarily significant for your wellbeing.

Truth be told, it's similarly as significant as eating well and working out.

Tragically, a ton can meddle with regular rest designs.

Individuals are presently resting short of what they did before, and rest quality has diminished too.

Here are reasons why adequate rest is significant.

1. Inadequate rest is connected to higher body weight

Inadequate rest is emphatically connected to weight gain.

Individuals with short rest span will in general, weigh essentially more than the individuals who get satisfactory rest.

Short rest length is one of the most grounded chance variables for weight.

In one broad survey study, kids and grown-ups with short rest length were 89% and 55% bound to create corpulence, separately.

The impact of rest on weight gain is accepted to be intervened by various elements, including hormones and inspiration to work out.

In case you're attempting to get thinner, getting quality rest is totally essential.

Synopsis

A short rest span is related with an expanded danger of weight increase and heftiness in the two kids and grown-ups.

2. High sleepers will, in general, eat less calories

Studies show that restless people have greater hunger and will, in general, eat more calories.

Lack of sleep upsets the day by day vacillations in craving hormones and is accepted to cause poor hunger guidelines.

This incorporates more significant levels of ghrelin, the hormone that animates craving, and decreased degrees of leptin, the hormone that stifles hunger.

Outline

Poor rest influences hormones that manage hunger. The individuals who get satisfactory rest will in general eat less calories than the individuals who don't.

3. Great rest can improve focus and efficiency

Rest is significant for different parts of mind work.

This incorporates perception, focus, efficiency, and execution.

These are adversely influenced by lack of sleep.

An investigation on clinical understudies gives a genuine model.

Understudies on a conventional timetable with expanded work long periods of over 24 hours made 36% more genuine clinical mistakes than assistants on a calendar that permitted more rest.

Another examination found that short rest can contrarily affect a few parts of mind capacity to a comparable degree as liquor inebriation.

Then again, great rest has been appeared to improve critical thinking aptitudes and upgrade memory execution of the two kids and grown-ups.

Rundown

Great rest can amplify critical thinking aptitudes and improve memory. Poor rest has been appeared to impede mind work.

4. Great rest can augment athletic execution

Rest has been said to improve athletic execution.

In an investigation on ballplayers, more extended rest appeared to fundamentally improve speed, exactness, response times, and mental prosperity.

Less rest length has likewise been related to poor exercise execution and useful restriction in more seasoned ladies.

An investigation in more than 2,800 ladies found that poor rest was connected to more slow strolling, lower hold quality, and more prominent trouble performing free exercises.

Synopsis

Longer rest has been appeared to improve numerous parts of athletic and physical execution.

5. Poor sleepers have a more serious danger of coronary illness and stroke

Rest quality and length can majorly affect numerous wellbeing hazard factors.

These are the components accepted to drive incessant illnesses, including coronary illness.

A survey of 15 investigations found that individuals who don't get enough rest are at far more serious danger of coronary illness or stroke than the individuals who rest 7–8 hours of the night.

Synopsis

Resting under 7–8 hours out of every night is connected to an expanded danger of coronary illness and stroke.

6. Rest influences glucose digestion and type 2 diabetes hazard

Exploratory rest limitation influences glucose and lessens insulin affectability.

In an investigation in sound youngsters, confining rest to 4 hours out of each night for 6 evenings straight caused indications of prediabetes.

These side effects settled following multi-week of expanded rest length.

Poor rest propensities are additionally firmly connected to antagonistic consequences for glucose in everybody.

Those dozing under 6 hours out of each night have more than once been demonstrated to be at an expanded danger of type 2 diabetes.

Synopsis

Lack of sleep can cause prediabetes in solid grown-ups in as meager as 6 days. Numerous investigations show a solid connection between short rest term and type 2 diabetes.

7. Poor rest is connected to misery

Emotional wellness issues, for example, despondency, are unequivocally connected to poor rest quality and dozing issue.

It's been assessed that 90% of individuals with wretchedness gripe about rest quality.

Poor rest is even connected with an expanded danger of death by self destruction.

Those with resting issue like a sleeping disorder or obstructive rest apnea likewise report altogether higher paces of melancholy than those without.

Poor dozing designs are emphatically connected to wretchedness, especially for those with a dozing issue.

8. Rest improves your resistant capacity

Indeed, even a little loss of rest has been appeared to disable insusceptible capacity.

One huge 2-week study observed the advancement of the regular cold in the wake of giving individuals nasal drops with the cool infection.

They found that the individuals who rested under 7 hours were right around multiple times bound to build up a cold than the individuals who dozed 8 hours or more.

On the off chance that you regularly get colds, guaranteeing that you get in any event 8 hours of rest for every night could be exceptionally useful. Eating more garlic can help also.

Rundown

Getting at any rate 8 hours of rest can improve your invulnerable capacity and help battle the normal virus.

9. Poor rest is connected to expanded aggravation

Rest can majorly affect aggravation in your body.

Truth be told, rest misfortune is known to enact bothersome markers of aggravation and cell harm.

Poor rest has been unequivocally connected to long haul aggravation of the stomach related tract, in clutters known as incendiary inside illness.

One examination saw that restless individuals with Crohn's illness were twice as liable to backslide as patients who rested soundly.

Specialists are in any event, prescribing rest assessment to help anticipate results in people with long haul incendiary issues.

Synopsis

Rest influences your body's provocative reactions. Poor rest is connected to fiery gut infections and can build your danger of ailment repeat.

10. Rest influences feelings and social connections

Rest misfortune diminishes your capacity to associate socially.

A few investigations affirmed this utilizing passionate facial acknowledgment tests.

One investigation found that individuals who hadn't dozed had a decreased capacity to perceive articulations of outrage and bliss.

Scientists accept that poor rest influences your capacity to perceive significant expressive gestures and procedure passionate data.

Outline

Lack of sleep may decrease your social aptitudes and capacity to perceive individuals' passionate articulations.

The main concern

Alongside nourishment and exercise, great rest is one of the mainstays of wellbeing.

You essentially can't accomplish ideal wellbeing without dealing with your rest.

Chapter 7: The State Of Meditation

Let's take a moment to consider meditation and its proven benefits for relaxation, stress management, and sleep before we dive into the exercise. I expect you to stick with this segment for some time. In it, you can find vital meaning, tips to get the most out of this book, and meditation's basic core principles. Without this simple understanding, you can find the practices of meditation challenging or confusing, and that is the last thing I want. Having a good understanding of the common meditation concepts can only make the activities and your experience more satisfying.

IT'S TIME TO RELAX

Do you ever feel like you need an extra hour? Even better, an extra day? Do you find that life moves faster than you wish?

Is it hard to keep up? Or like you can keep up, but there's not enough time to do the things you want actually to do? Were you preoccupied with the future? Do you feel nervous, irritated, tired, or a combination of all three? Do not worry if any of these feelings resonate with you— they are all too prevalent in our modern society. Our entrenched personal expectations and rising external commitments continually propel us forward. So while we like to think that the TV shows are binge-watching and the gadgets that we are hooked to help us relax, they only serve to amuse us (at best) and add to our overwhelm.

This endless cycle, which I call "over-stress, under-rest," sometimes leaves us too awake to sleep, but too exhausted to be successful in doing something. Chronic stress and sleep deprivation in many countries around the world are, in fact, epidemics now. This process can lead to serious health problems, addictions, and strained relationships. We could be faced with years of blurred, senseless repetition if we don't make improvements, but life does not have to be like this. Clear, available meditation practices will help you relax, find relaxation, and enhance the quality and length of your sleep, as you will learn in the coming chapters.

MEDITATION AND RELAXATION

Evidence continues to show that meditation provides essential benefits to our mental and physical health by generating a positive change cycle—better sleep leads to improved mood, increased emotional endurance, a more relaxed feeling, and better sleep. This section shows the proven benefits you can expect from doing the meditations in this book. Improvement in all of these areas will affect your quality of life significantly over the long term.

Stress Reduction

Many studies have shown that meditation reduces stress. A 2014 study by JAMA Internal Medicine, involving more than 3,500 participants in various studies, found that daily meditation brought about changes in many forms of negative psychological stress, including anxiety, depression, and pain. Also, a study at the University of Wisconsin–Madison in 2013 found that an eight-week therapy program had diminished participants due to stress-induced inflammation. Besides, an analysis of over 600 research papers representing almost 1,300 participants in 2014 concluded that meditation reduces stress, especially among those with the highest rates. And that is just the start.

Restful Sleep

The melatonin reserves, a hormone linked to restful sleep, are often depleted by stress. Meditation both decreases stress and stimulates the body's natural processes for generating melatonin, which means it can help you fall asleep faster and sleep longer. A 2012 study by a team at Rutgers University found that in some participants, meditation increased melatonin levels by 300 percent.

Quiet Meditation

Anecdotal evidence has shown that even short periods of meditation can have the hormonal and neurological benefits of two to three times the same amount of sleep—meaning you can meditate for 20 minutes and feel as relaxed as you would after an hour of sleep, without being tired. It is not to suggest, of course, that you can meditate rather than sleep (though some devoted practitioners claim that they need less sleep as a result of regular meditation over long periods). You do need your sleep, but you can reap many of the advantages of deep sleep with quick bursts of meditation and get better sleep (when you're not meditating).

Heightened Awareness

In addition to increasing the awareness of what is happening outside of the body and mind in the present moment, meditation helps to improve the perception of the feelings, emotions, and causes of stress and anxiety within your body and mind. This increased understanding has many benefits for both the immediate and long-term.

For example, if you have unhealthy behaviors that are caused by physical or emotional stress, meditation will help you develop both stressor sensitivity and default response. This sensitivity can give you greater control of your choices. For example, if you feel like the 3 pm slump, that extra cup of coffee, you can choose not to have in the afternoon. And you can pause before bed in the evening and decide not to have a bowl of chocolate ice cream. Both of these cautious choices will increase your sleep quality and duration and therefore decrease your stress. Increased awareness also increases the sensations of joy, thankfulness, and wonder. The more conscious you are of the good things around you and within you, the more you enjoy them.

Decreased Blood Pressure

The American Heart Association reviewed several meditation studies and their impact on blood pressure and discovered some evidence that meditation may help to reduce blood pressure. There is an established physiological reaction to stress relief, which we know supports reflection. Meditation should not, however, be used as a primary tool for treating hyperstress. When you have questions about elevated blood pressure, speak with your doctor about it. Meanwhile, I realize that meditation does not cause any harm and can actually be useful in a meaningful way.

Peace and Calm

When we go through our busy days, meeting people and circumstances that make us feel distracted, disappointed, upset, sad, jealous, or irritated is unavoidable, but what if you would respond to those stimuli differently—or not respond at all? What if you only witnessed the crime, the annoyance, the irritant, yet have not internalized it? Chances are, the moment—and the corresponding moments in the day—

would make everyone involved much friendlier.

Practicing meditation helps you cultivate the ability to understand that the response is not the emotional stressor or the cause. They're separate, so your reaction is under your control—you can choose to let or not let something stress you out. You're never going to be able to change all the crazy things that happen in life, but you can change how it affects you. Developing this skill through daily meditation helps alleviate stress in real-time so that you can conserve your strength for more essential and pleasurable things.

Chapter 8: Induction

At this point in the audio, I invite you to make yourself as comfortable as possible in your bed. Please have all the light's turned off and distractions put away. You have already put in a full, hard day of work. Think of sleeping sound and comfortable through the night as a reward for working so hard.

How was your day today? Were you productive? How did you feel?

I want you to think about these questions as you settle further into the bed. Gently tuck yourself under the cover, and we will begin our journey. Ready?

Inhale deeply. Hold onto that breath for a moment, and then let it go. To begin, I am going to lead you through an induction script for self-hypnosis. By allowing yourself to slip into this state of mind, it will help you let go of any stress you may be holding onto, even if it is in your subconscious. I am going to help you tap into these emotions so you can let them go and sleep like you never have before.

All of us are stressed. Honestly, who can sleep when they are worried? In this state of mind, you probably feel too alert to even think about sleeping. When you are stressed, the adrenal glands in your body release adrenaline and cortisol. Both of these hormones keep you awake and stop you from falling asleep.

In the audio to follow, we will go over letting go of your worries, even if it is just for the night. You are in a safe place right now. Anything you need to get done can wait until tomorrow. It is important you take this time for yourself. We all need a break from our responsibilities at some point or another. I invite you now to take another deep breath so we can focus on what is important right now; sleep.

To start, I would like you to close your eyes gently. As you do this, wiggle slightly until your body feels comfortable in your bed. When you find your most comfortable position, it is time to begin breathing.

As you focus on your breath, remind yourself to breathe slow and deep. Feel as the air fills your lungs and release it in a comfortable way. Feel as your body relaxes further under the sheets. You begin to feel a warm glow, wrapping your whole body in a comfortable blanket.

Before you let go into a deep hypnotic state, listen carefully to the words I am saying at this moment.

Everything is going to happen automatically.

At this moment, there is nothing you need to focus on. You will have no control over what happens next in our session. But you are okay with that. At this moment, you are warm and safe. You are preparing your body for a full night's rest and letting go of any thoughts you may have. There is no need to think of the future or the past. The only thing that matters right now is your comfort, your breath, and the incredible sleep you are about to experience.

Now, feel as the muscles around your eyes begin to relax. I invite you to continue breathing deeply and bring your attention to your eyes. They are beginning to feel heavy and relaxed. Your eyes worked hard for you today. They watched as you worked, they kept you safe as you walked around, and they showed other people you were paying attention to them as you spoke. Thank your eyes at this moment and allow them to rest for the night so they will be prepared for tomorrow.

Your breath is coming easy and free now. Soon, you will enter a hypnotic trance with no effort. This trance will be deep, peaceful, and safe. There is nothing for your conscious mind to do at this moment. There are no activities you need to complete. Allow for your subconscious mind to take over and do the work for you.

This trance will come automatically. Soon, you will feel like you are dreaming. Allow yourself to relax and give in to my voice. All you need to focus on is my voice.

You are doing wonderfully. Without noticing, you have already changed your rate of breath. You are breathing easy and free. There is no thought involved. Your body knows exactly what you need to do, and you can relax further into your subconscious mind.

Now, you are beginning to show signs of drifting off into this peaceful hypnotic trance. I invite you to enjoy the sensations as your subconscious mind takes over and listens to the words I am speaking to you. It is slowly becoming less important for you to listen to me. Your subconscious listens, even as I begin to whisper.

You are drifting further and further away. You are becoming more relaxed and more comfortable. At this moment, nothing is bothering you. Your inner mind is listening to me, and you are beginning to realize that you don't care about slipping into a deep trance.

This peaceful state allows you to be comfortable and relaxed. Being hypnotized is pleasant and enjoyable. This is beginning to feel natural for you. Each time I hypnotize you, it becomes more enjoyable than the time before.

You will enjoy these sensations. You are comfortable. You are peaceful. You are completely calm.

As we progress through the relaxing exercises, you will learn something new about yourself. You are working gently to develop your own sleep techniques without even knowing you are developing them in the first place.

On the count of three, you are going to slip completely into your subconscious state. When I say the number three, your brain is going to take over, and you will find yourself in the forest. This forest is peaceful, calm, and serene. It is safe and comfortable, much like your bed at this moment. Take a deep breath in and exhale...you are ready for your journey.

One...

Two...

Three...

Welcome to the peaceful forest.

Before we begin, I want you to inhale deeply and hold onto the breath for three seconds. Once you have held the breath for three seconds, exhale slowly. You can breathe on my count. Ready?

Breathe in...two...three...four...hold...two...three...four...exhale...two...three...four.

Wonderful. You are doing a fantastic job. Let's do that a few more times.

Breathe in...two...three...four...hold...two...three...four...exhale...two...three...four.

Breathe in…two…three…four…hold…two…three…four…exhale…two…three…four

Breathe in…two…three…four…hold…two…three…four…exhale…two…three…four

As you inhale, try to bring more oxygen into your body with nice, deep breaths. As you exhale, feel as your body relaxes more and more into the bed. Breathing comes easy and free for you. As you continue to focus on your breath, you are becoming more peaceful and calmer without even realizing it.

As we continue, you do not care how relaxed you are. You are happy in the state of mind. You do not have a care in the world. Your subconscious mind is always aware of the words I am saying to you. As we go along, it is becoming less important for you to listen to my voice.

Your inner mind is receiving everything I tell you. Your conscious mind is relaxed and peaceful. As you find your own peace of mind, we will begin to explore this forest you have found yourself in, together.

Now, I want you to imagine you are laying near a stream in this beautiful and peaceful forest. It is a sunny, warm summer day. As you lay comfortably in the grass beside this stream, you feel a warm breeze, gently moving through your hair. Inhale deep and experience how fresh and clean this air is. Inhale again and exhale. Listen carefully as the stream flows beside you. A quiet whoosh noise, filling your ears and relaxing you even further.

It is becoming less and less important for you to listen to me. Your subconscious mind takes hold and listens to everything I am saying. All you need to do is enjoy the beautiful nature around you. The sunlight shines through the trees and kisses your skin gently. The birds begin to sing a happy tune. You smile, feeling yourself become one with nature.

Each time you exhale, I want to imagine your whole body relaxing more. You are becoming more at ease. As you do this, I want you to begin to use your imagination. You are lying on the grass. It is located in a green meadow with the sun shining down on you. The sun is not hot, but a comfortable warm.

Imagine that there are beautiful flowers blooming everywhere around you. Watch as the flowers move gently in the breeze. Their scents waft toward your nose as you inhale deeply and exhale.

When you are ready, I want you to imagine that you begin to stand up. As you do this, you look over your left shoulder gently, and you see a mountain near the edge of the beautiful meadow. You decide that you would like to take a trip up to the top of the mountain to see this beautiful view from a different angle.

As you begin to walk, you follow the stream. Imagine gently bending over and placing your hand not the cool, rushing water. As you look upon the water, imagine how clean and cool this water is. The stream flows gently across your fingers and it relaxes you.

When you are ready, we will head toward the mountain again. As you grow closer to the mountain, the birds begin to chirp. Inhale deep and imagine how the pine trees smell around you. Soon, you begin to climb the mountain at a comfortable pace.

You are enjoying the trip. It is wonderful to be outside with this beautiful nature, taking in all the sights and sounds. Now, you are already halfway up the mountain. The meadow grows smaller as you climb higher, but you are not afraid. The scene is beautiful from up here, and you are happy at this moment.

As you reach the top, take a deep breath and give yourself a pat on the back for your accomplishment. Take a look down on the meadow and see how small the trees look.

The breeze is blowing your hair around gently, and the sun continues to shine down on the top of your head. Imagine that you are taking a seat at the very top of the mountain. You close your eyes in your mind's eye and take a few moments to appreciate this nature. You wish you could always be this relaxed.

When you take your life into your own hands, you will be able to. This is why we are here. Of course, you may be here because you want to sleep, but you can't do that truly unless you learn how to let go of your stress. Through guided meditation and exercises within this audio, you will learn how to become a better version of yourself. I am here to help you every step of the way.

Soon, we will work on deepening your trance. You are beginning to relax further into the meditation and are opening your heart and soul to the practice. Remember that you are safe, and you are happy to be here.

Chapter 9: What Is Meditation?

These are common questions that people began to learn about meditation. In the West, the word meditation means a concentrated state of mind in serious reflection. The Latin root of the word meditation, mederi, means "to heal". So "What is meditation?". You should not complicate the answer, simply understand: Meditation is an approach that anyone can use to help them cope with medical problems, stress, and anxiety by way of thought, contemplation, and reflection.

Origin

Finding the origin of meditation may be quite difficult. Meditation is deep-rooted in Asia, and countries like China, India and Japan are practicing it for thousands of years. Tribes in South India had developed Tantric Meditation about 15 thousand years back. Tantric meditation was in common use those days. So, we can put forward that concept of meditation emerged from Asia and took various forms in all over the world. Other views about the origin of meditation claims that it originated from the human being's curiosity for the purpose of men, purpose of the universe and to find God by looking inside the self to realize the nature and its existence.

Historical Perspectives

All historians have consensus over the points that, meditation has evolved during unknown ancient times and that; it was not practiced in such a way in which it is practiced today. Taoists started practicing meditation during 500 to 600 BC. Buddhists also started using meditation in the same era. In history, Buddha is one of the greatest promoters of meditation. He was the one to teach meditation in Asia during 500 BC. Buddha has introduced the basic forms of meditation, and all the world adapted and transformed these meditation techniques according to their needs and purposes. The important point to note here is that, Eastern countries were the origin of meditation and getting relief through various meditation techniques. West had adapted this culture from East. During 20th century, Western researchers conducted researches on meditation and came to know about its physical and psychological benefits. Since then, they are using meditation as a wide spread practice in their culture. Western population widely practiced meditation for peace of mind and to get relief from daily life stresses. Nowadays, a downfall has been observed in practices of meditation, and reason is lack of time.

Many years ago meditation was considered something not just meant for modern people, but now it has become very popular with all types of people. Published scientific and medical evidence has proved its benefits.

Meditation encompasses a variety of practices that are somewhat different, while holding to the basic principles of consideration and quiet thought to bring about a state of rumination. Various types of meditation that are recognized include prayer, Zen, Taoist, mindfulness, and Buddhist. Some methods of meditation may require the body being absolutely still or to be moved with controlled deliberation, while other types allow for free movement of the body. While the methods are different, the end goal of all types of meditation lead to a mind that is quieted and free from stress by the use of quiet contemplation and reflection.

Chances are in your life you have unknowingly experienced moments in a purely meditative state. The odds are that when this occurred, you found yourself outside in nature. In nature we more easily find resonance with a deeper more real aspect of ourselves which often comes alive in the natural environment.

Perhaps it occurred while relaxing on a beach watching the hypnotic like waves repetitively washing ashore or possibly noticing the invisible wind rustle leaves on a tree as warming sunlight bathed your face. If you recall during these moments, you found a completely relaxed feeling immerse your entire being because you were free of distracting thoughts. This is what being in "the moment" is all about. It is as if your mind tunes into the higher natural frequencies of life which for the most part, are virtually non-existent inside buildings and such. Yet, with focus, proper intentions and processes we can escape these limitations imposed in man-made environments. Of course meditation can be greatly enhanced when it is practical in natural surroundings.

The whole concept of meditation takes on various identities depending what an individual's intention is while performing a chosen meditation. Some may want physical or mental relief, others, answers or directions for a better life. Either way, choices are clearly individualized. Find yours since this goes a long way in helping you along the path aided with a unique, personalized purpose. Define it for you! To begin a meditation, a few simple rules are universally accepted. These generally are-

Posture is important in that you must be comfortable.

Preferably this is with your back upright and your spine to your head straight.

Normally a seated position on the ground is preferred with hands in your lap; it can also be done in a chair. Lying down initially is not suggested as your body can assume a sleep mode.

Activate the heart-mind connection which provides an initial thought-clearing mode.

Do not attempt to suppress these thoughts. Acknowledge them. Briefly as thoughts arise, dismiss them by surrounding any with the six heart virtues of: appreciation, compassion, forgiveness, humility, valor, and understanding. Another very powerful technique is to apply unconditional love (without a judgment position) to any thoughts that may arise, release them and return focus to your breathing.

Close your eyes gently, relax your jaw and facial muscles.

Do a "body scan" looking for any muscle tension that may exist releasing any found. Continue relaxing now for a few moments allowing your body to become comfortable. Be observant of bodily tension arising. The key is to physically relax.

Slowly evacuate your lungs completely.

Gently inhale and exhale through your nostrils with a deep (from the belly) rhythmic cycle filling your lungs to capacity and expelling the air completely. Slow, long in and out breaths are ideal. Pausing momentarily at the end of each in and out breath. Focus on the feeling and sounds during the entire cycle.

Break away from distractions.

Turn off the outside electrical/technological intrusions like phones, computers, TV's etc. A quiet, calm and peaceful place is preferred. At first, commit 10 minutes or more with no interruption.

Steadily and incrementally increase the time duration spent in your practice.

As the moments of time lengthen between arising thoughts, you are now well on the way to higher levels of meditation. Remind yourself to notice and appreciate the beneficial by-products you have regained.

How Meditation Works

Mindfulness meditation is a scientifically proven exercise for your brain. Just like you need to exercise your body by running and lifting weights, you also need to exercise your mind.

We are constantly bombarded by thoughts and feelings inside our heads, day and night, so much so that we don't even realize it's happening. We flip out and get angry, get crippled by anxiety, or spiral into depression. Those states come from negative thoughts that pop into our heads. Most people are unaware of these thoughts and react to them instantly. Someone cuts you off in traffic, and you shout in anger and think about it all day afterward. Or if social anxiety is your problem, you may be constantly worrying about what other people think about you and create stories in your mind of how others will negatively judge you. We become owned by these thoughts and feelings. But we need not be.

That's what the practice of meditation aims to do. You simply sit quietly, focus on your breath, and try to quiet your mind. (Which will be impossible.) You will inevitably have tons of thoughts popping into your mind, but that's okay. That's the purpose of meditation: to observe your thoughts, then dismiss them and return to your breath. Realize that just because you have a thought, it doesn't mean you have to react emotionally to the thought. You can let negative thoughts go. They are just thoughts.

The point of meditation isn't to have no thoughts; it's to notice when a thought pops into your head, then dismiss it and return to focus on your breath. Meditation is a practice to learn to ignore negative thoughts.

Of course, this is extremely difficult to do. Most people have been unconsciously accepting every thought that pops into their heads without realizing it for their entire lives. Your thoughts affect your emotions. So if you accept every negative thought that pops into your head, you will inevitably experience negative emotions with no control over them. However, you can separate yourself from your thoughts and gain control over your emotional state.

That's the goal of meditation: to gain control over your thoughts, so you are not clouded by emotions and can see reality more clearly. Naturally, bad things will still happen in life. You will still get angry, anxious, scared, and sad, but with the practice of meditation, you can realize more quickly that you are angry or scared, then think about why, and realize how those feelings may or may not be serving you. There are certainly times in life you should be angry or scared, but oftentimes those feelings are caused by irrational thoughts, and you'd be better off by letting those feelings go.

For instance, if someone cuts you off in traffic, or says something nasty about you on the internet, or a political news report gets your blood boiling, you will ruminate on those things for the rest of the day (or longer). But ruminating about trivial matters that are out of your control will not help you in any way. Meditation helps you to be conscious of your thoughts, recognize when you're ruminating, then be able to stop and return to the present—focus on the things you can control in life.

Meditation has specifically helped me cope with anxiety. Anxiety is like getting constant pop-up ads inside your head (except the ads are negative thoughts). Meditation is your mental ad blocker. It's a practice of training yourself to delete the ads as soon as they pop up, instead of clicking every one or unconsciously ruminating on negative thought-patterns all day. When you feel anxious, it's often a constant barrage of negative thoughts and never-ending rumination. One pop-up leads to another ad, and you find yourself in a rabbit hole of anxiety and overthinking. The goal of meditation is to recognize a thought (any thought) as soon as it pops up, and instead of following it, simply forget it and return to focusing on your breath.

Meditation is often called a practice because it is just that—practice. A baseball pitcher must practice throwing in order to succeed in the game. So must we practice mindfulness to succeed in the game that is our entire life. You practice mindfulness deliberately for 10-20 minutes of meditation each day, so that you can be naturally more mindful the rest of the day. Through the practice of mindfulness you learn to control your thoughts and emotions, to be less reactive, less stressed, less anxious, and more calm and content. You don't meditate for the moment you are meditating; you do it to prepare your mind for later—for when some jerk cuts you off in traffic, so you will be more in control of your thoughts and emotions and won't lose your temper. Or if you are in an anxiety-inducing social setting, you may still feel fear, but you can be better being able to ignore the fear and return to a calm state.

You can't control your genes or the environment, but you can control how you respond to those factors. Eventually you'll realize, "Oh, this is just my hormones triggering a fear response in my brain, resulting in an increased heart rate. Due to my genetics programmed by hundreds of thousands of years of evolution, my brain assumes this situation is a threat, but it's actually not that dangerous, so I can ignore those feelings." With enough practice, you can have that realization instantly and immediately ignore the negative thought or feeling when it arises.

Chapter 10: A Full Guide To The Art And Benefits Of Meditation

Since time immemorial, we have been hearing about how important it is to let go at times and leave all your physical ties with the world to achieve peace. This has been summed up shortly as the path to ultimate salvation. As it would happen, in today's busy and bustling times, the quest for peace and salvation has even become more relevant and resonant. Incidentally, the Eastern philosophies of India and China prize mental peace which can be accomplished through the path of serious meditation. Here is a detailed guide to the origins, techniques and benefits of meditation for all the starters and beginners.

The Origins

It was in the fertile Indus Valley, currently a part of Sindh which lies across both India and Pakistan, where the art of meditation actually took shape. The Indus Valley Civilization was known as the Harappa Civilization and the ruins of the ancient regime included wall paintings as well as the Mohen Ja Daro tanks and bathing wells. In the wall paintings, evidence lies of how ancient techniques of meditation had been used by the people who lived in the period of 5000 to 3500 BCE. There are detailed drawings and illustrations of people sitting in varying postures and positions, which are today called by yogis as Asanas'.

The Indian scriptures and ancient relics found in other archaeological excavations go a long way in proving that the art of meditation, today called in a variant as Yoga, was indeed a regular part of life of people in ancient India. Long before people found that meditation decreases depression, anxiety and insomnia, people in ancient India were already using meditation also as a form of corrective surgery. According to them, meditation helped sooth the nerves and regulate good circulation in the muscles and tissues of the body. These were some reasons behind meditation being so common in the ancient days of the country.

The Adaptations Of Meditation

While it is in ancient India that meditation first took its definite shape, it must be acknowledged that the future religions and faiths did a great job by adapting the art of meditation in their own way or the other. Buddhism was the first one to do this. Their practice of meditation was closely modelled on how Lord Buddha had meditated sitting under the Bodhi tree for enlightenment. Ever since then, meditation has become a crucial theme for Chinese and other Oriental cultures. Islam adapted it in the form of the regular prayers which were also a variant of meditation in the form of prayer.

Islam also encouraged the rise of Sufism, a full-throated liberal sect of Muslims, whose belief is that Allah resides in human beings and the love of human beings is the love of Allah. Sufis are well known for the Dervish dance, a trance-like dance in which the performers enter into a trance-like state of meditation. It has been unanimously said that this dance form is one in which the dancers and the performers actually feel closer to the God on a spiritual level and attain great enlightenment and peace of mind as well. The Dervish dance has since become popular.

Meditation In Christianity

Meditation is also an integral part of the Christian religion. The fact has often been debated widely by many theorists. In fact, the truth is that the Christian philosophers claim that there are certain worship methods in the religion that can be classified as forms of meditation. One is that there is a common technique of worshipping the Christ by spending many waking hours lost in contemplation. This phase of introspection is often considered as a more pedantic form of meditation. Equally pedantic is the method of reading rosary beads, which is also similar to the method of reading beads in Islam and Judaism as well.

Meditation In Judaism

Ever heard of Kabala? Well, if you haven't heard of this insanely popular term among the youngsters, well then better know about it now. First of all, its real name is Kabbalah which means that you better take its mystical nature rather serious as well. The main technique of the Kabbalah is that you need to recite some of the main prayers that had been said first by the God Moses in the presence of the Angel. These prayers will help to act like any other form of meditation and bring down all your troubles.

The Spread Of Meditation

Western countries like UK and America remained largely immune from the allure of meditation for the simple reason that they had not embraced the stricter forms of religion then. But thanks to the relentless forays of famed yogi and Indian scholar and orator Swami Vivekananda, the philosophy of ancient meditation came to the American shores in the first half of the 20th Century. In one of his typically elaborate and well-known speeches, Vivekananda, soon to be one of trademark reformers of the age, talked largely about the wonders that meditation and other Asian cultural touchstones could do for the Western populace.

In the 50s, owing to the Beat literature movement in America, the concept of Buddhist Zen philosophy further became popular. Many youngsters of the era soon started embarking on the path of Zen and this was chronicled by author Jack Kerouac in his famous novel The Dharma Burns' faithfully as an alternative lifestyle as well. In the 60s, India's Maharishi Mahesh Yogi attracted the clout of young actors and musicians including actress Mia Farrow as well as the famous English rock and roll band The Beatles. Together, with such celebrities to drive the cause of meditation, it became a sensation in the Western culture as well.

Why Technique Is Important

Most people have the sordid misconception that meditation is all about sitting quietly in one place and closing your eyes and all that jazz. This is a serious misconception that can even ruin the effects of meditation. It should be understood that meditation has its own schools of thoughts, all of which preach varied ways and techniques for meditating and attaining the rare thing called Nirvana. Below are some of the main techniques in vogue in today's fast and furious world.

Transcendental Meditation

One of the most popular methods and doctrines on meditation is that which was pioneered by the famed guru Maharishi Mahesh Yogi. The Transcendental Method preaches that the people, who are meditating, should not concentrate their efforts on chanting prayers and mantras or on their respiratory activities. Rather, it merely focuses on how to discover your inner calm. The person may be required to concentrate his mental effort in removing troublesome thoughts and concentrating only on pleasurable experiences, thoughts and visions. This type of meditation decreases depression, anxiety and insomnia effectively as it sooths the body and the mind completely.

Buddhist Meditation

The Buddhist doctrine of meditation varies sharply from the Transcendental method which had been recommended by the people. This means that the Buddhist doctrine has recommended that the people who will meditate will concentrate and focus their efforts on mainly their respiratory processes sternly. The entire process is to sit calmly and to make a concentrated effort to listen and feel to your breathing rhythms and movements in a concentrated effort. Doing this will help to sooth the mind as well as the body and you will also feel quite relaxed and calm.

But there is another method of doing the Buddhist doctrine of meditation. In this method, the Buddhists have to sit for a prolonged period of time under the shade or preferably in the darkness. Doing this involves shutting out the other foreign thoughts from the mind and getting freed from the pressures of everyday life and work as well. This type of meditation also involves concentrating on regular happiness and little joys and bringing your inner calm into the picture so as to make yourself enlightened and wise as well.

Yoga

Yoga is one of the most famous variants of the art of meditation, which was prescribed by the Indian doctrine of meditation as well. The basic difference between Yoga and other variants is that Yoga is also a form of leisurely and flexible exercise which makes your body feel fit. This means that other forms of meditation might prescribe only physical and mental peace. Yoga goes ahead and suggests that the person should try to keep the body flexible, agile and active so as to achieve a perfect harmony of mental and physical peace and well-being. This is the main philosophy behind yoga.

Yoga has been taught to Indians since the ancient ages and it has been one of the main gifts of the Indian civilization to the West. The usual techniques of Yoga are called as postures or Asanas'. Some of these asanas are challenging postures which can be achieved through tremendous feats of the physical abilities. Many of these postures can be achieved mainly to bring about a high level of internal physical flexibility and mental concentration. Some of the other postures recommend the people to stay calm and introspect as to gain as much mental peace than possible.

The Benefits Of Meditation

Now that you know about the basic concepts and fundamentals about meditation, you need to also know about the benefits that meditation would offer to you. First of all, meditation is widely recognized as a superb and reliable remedy for the problem of physical and mental stress. This means that it works great for the mind by soothing it and removing all sources of worry and other obstacles as well. By doing regular meditation, one does feel quite distressed, confident and assured of handling bigger challenges. One also begins to feel positive and optimistic as well.

Anxiety and Insomnia

It is indeed true that meditation decreases depression, anxiety and insomnia. Anxiety means a constant state of panic, distress and trouble over a lingering thought or idea in the mind. A lot of people fall prey to panic attacks and fits owing to an overload of anxiety. Worse, many people also become vulnerable to cardiovascular problems as a result of anxiety. Therefore, by meditating, one is able to shut out the outer thoughts and concentrate only on the good thoughts and pleasurable feelings and sentiments. Thus, anxiety can be solved with meditation.

Remedy For Insomnia

Insomnia is the syndrome of lack of sleep. Mostly, it stems from the fact that people are unable to sleep because of some underlying stress or some major psychological reason as well. Insomnia has several remedies like sleeping pills or even green tea and so on. However, insomnia can be suitably addressed by the solution of meditation. In the case of meditation, it helps to cleanse your mind of bad thoughts and ugly feelings. This helps in the case of making the body sufficiently at peace and you will be able to fall into deep sleep without feeling any problems at all.

Blood Pressure

Among the physical benefits of the meditation techniques is the fact that the basic meditation method will also help to bring down crucial levels of blood pressure and other such level high things. Blood pressure comes down when your circulatory and respiratory processes are improved in the path of meditation. Also, with better blood pressure and more mental peace, your optimism also improves and you may also be protected from cardiovascular problems in the future as well. This means that you will be saved from the threats of cholesterol and heart attack and diabetes as well.

The Final Word

As you can see, meditation is an ancient concept which originated in the Indian civilization in the golden ancient ages. With time, it has been suitably modified and assimilated by all the major religions and communities in the world. Even the Western cultures and communities have suitably embraced the art of meditation which has helped to solve all the mental and physical health problems. So, it is up to you to warm up to meditation techniques as well. You need to learn all about them and you also will benefit from meditation in a large way.

Chapter 11: Your Divine Self

The divine self is the inner life force. This is your true motivation for living. The divine self-powers you and cause you to wonder. It is the light at your core that chose to be incarnate a certain point in time.

The divine self is always aware. It has been thinking and aware since you were born in this lifetime and every other lifetime. The physical realm and body that we dwell in is just what holds your higher self.

You chose to be here, and that's why you are here. This energy force of awareness and life provides you with lessons that have to be learned, and exchanges need to be made that you are only about to do as a human.

It might seem like the rules of incarnation, birth, and living in this busy world would prevent us from knowing our diving self which lives within our core. This doesn't have to be true. You can choose it to be a different way.

We can acknowledge our divine core and start to draw ourselves even closer to our higher being.

The first thing you have to do is to embrace your divine self.

Let your mind shut off as you quiet and calm yourself.

Get rid of distractions. No music, clocks, telephones, children, lawnmowers, television, or radios.

Sit comfortably and chose a mirror or candle.

If you chose a candle, stare into the flame. If you want to use a mirror, start at it and look over your entire face. Make sure you don't look into your eyes, and don't allow the flame to cause your eyes to go out of focus

Stay aware of yourself. Remain in your body and keep yourself relaxed. Keep your eyes focused.

The candle flame represents the light that is all life force. Everything that is alive is powered by light. All things that are real is perceivable by the absorption and reflection of light. Light is all that is.

The mirror reflects an image of self that is both avoided and embraced.

We stay away from it because we tend to want to compare it to beauty or perfect that we expect to find within the natural world. We stay away from imperfections of the body because they make use think we are unlovable and unworthy.

People don't realize that life is about the imperfections. Conscious energy is perfect and wants to be incarnate, so it can experience the sorrow and joy that is a reality. It wants to experience sorrow and joy that is imperfect and learn how to send our unconditional love in spite of these sorrows and imperfections.

This is the only time where you can learn true lessons and become closer to integrating with the All. The All is the Source or Creator. It isn't female or male but just is. All is presented the same way as everything else; it comes from its source. This means that everyone, awareness, and light is constantly present and everyone is siblings in this Light Family.

Something that we tend to miss is that the things and people that we assume are perfect have actually been changed to appear perfect and they're in no way natural. The thought of natural perfection is just a lie

Another reason we embrace self is the ego; everybody understands that we have a body, and this body contains a shape, face, mouth, nose, and eyes. We believe this to be the truth because we are about to see and feel it.

When a person looks in a mirror, they will likely only see a physical thing, something that is made up of matter, like a candle or match. We may be matter, and we do decay and die, but there's more. We can feel anger, love, cry, make things with our hands, celebrate religions, reproduce, stay up late to think, and make choices.

Are we just matter? Are we not anything more like a personality incarnate or a spirit?

Thoughts and personality aren't just a physical function. They may be powered by a physical function, but this is only a bridge between you body and spirit. Gas powers a car through combustion which changes the gases state. The brain works to convert the spirit, but we need the spirit to fuel our lives. When our engines becomes clogged, we only have to look for a neglected spirit to find the reason.

Being looking at your reflection in the mirror as not something that is just bone and flesh, but also as a spiritual being that moves within your body. Then you will develop the connection that you have to things that are beyond the physical realm.

Take a moment to look at your reflection. Notice your body's light and the life glow that surrounds it.

While doing this either with the mirror or candle, embrace the energy of creation, the light of life, and your connection to it all. Say this affirmation, "I believe in myself. I know it because I feel it in me. I can see it in my life."

Repeat this and don't be mindless. Repeat as you feel this truth in your heart. Take note of the divine energy and the connection with the universe and the buzz of creation on your skin.

Continue to repeat this, or change it to suit you. Think about the divine self and then try to make contact with the manifesting self

Make sure you stay open to the divine self and keep the heart open to be able to communicate with the higher being and see how your life happens.

Do this with the cycle of the moon. This is best during a new moon. Continue doing this for as long as you feel you need to so that you can build up your relationship with your higher being, and to come closer to understanding.

At the mystical heart of all religions is the higher self. Understanding the higher self is the most important thing that anyone can have.

The higher self is seen as a relationship with the evolving self on the Chart of Your Divine Self. I show many cosmic truths that were discovered by great mystics of the West and East.

The Chart has three parts that can be called your identity's trinity.

There is an upper figure where a sphere of light resides. The Hindus call this Brahma. Buddhists call it Dharmakaya and Christians think of it as the Heavenly Father. It is God's spirit that has been individualized for everyone.

Your higher self is surrounded by seven spheres that make up your body. These spheres of energy contain all your good works. This is your cosmic bank account.

Your body has spheres of cosmic consciousness that include seven planes of heaven and seven spheres of awareness that correspond with the seven days of creation, the seven Archangels, the seven Elohim, and the seven colors that come from the white light that is the Father.

These seven ways lead to seven paths that go back to the Source. The lords of the seven rays are masters who teach on these paths.

Your higher self is a part of you right now. It will never be removed. It is not separate from you in space or time. The only separation that you have from your higher self is your consciousness, your limitations, and the vibrations you have accumulated from this life and previous ones that are less than your highest qualities.

Between the light above and the soul below is the higher self. The higher self is a part of you that translates an imperfect soul into perfection. It is a portion of you that is real and can stand within the presence of your God.

Some Christians refer to your higher self as the inner heart of the man.

It is your higher self that helps you come through your evolutions and all your experiences in space and time.

Depending on your religion, you can think of this higher self as a guardian angel, voice of conscience, your inner guru, and of course your closest friend.

What the Chart shows is that all of us has a higher self and everyone is destined to be one with the higher self. It doesn't matter if we call it Atman, Tao, Buddha, or Christ.

Your soul evolves on a spiritual path in space and time. It is part of the mortal you, but it can become immortal.

The violet flame is a presence that surrounds you. This flame is an energy that has a high frequency and forgives. It is a spiritual alchemy.

There is a protective white light known as God around the violet flame. We apply the spoken word to call forth the light as protection. It will seal our chakras and aura from the weight of darkness.

The white light that descends from God to the higher self is a silver cord or the umbilical cord. It is the lifeline that connects you to the Spirit.

This silver cord nourishes a radiant flame of God that is closed inside the secret chamber in the heart. This is a threefold flame that carries the attributes of love, wisdom, and power.

It is a very spiritual flame that is about 1/16th of an inch and focused in the body at heart. It is a sacred fire that God has moved from his heart to yours.

Your soul's evolution is ascended to the light, fulfill your mission, balance your karma, and grow in self-mastery.

The end of your incarnations is becoming the real self so you can return to the spiritual dimension that is your real home. By paying attention to your spiritual path, the figures on the chart that are separated due to a limited consciousness will eventually become one.

You can attain a union with God.

Chapter 12: The "Constant Change" Meditation

Everything around is constantly changing, forever evolving. Just think about the 4 seasons of nature, the alternation between day and night or the unstoppable rhythm of time. You see, when we have a scar in our soul due to a past event, we tend to think that it will be with us for the rest of time. This would be true if we were static creatures, but being created by nature we follow the universal law of evolution.

Everything is evolving on a large and small scale. On a large scale, we started our evolution millions of years ago, when the first organic cells started forming. On a small scale, each and everyone of us goes through a personal evolution, that goes from the moment they were born to the moment of their death. Well, actually some traditions and cultures believes that the journey does not begin or end with life, but that is outside our interest for the time being.

What is important to understand, in order to really grasp the benefits of this practice, is that what we feel today will not last forever, even if we think so. This goes for good and bad feelings, without distinctions. I know that if you have just gone through a difficult period of your life, you might think you will never fully recover. I hope this practice will give you that extra hope that it is possible and that you are already on the path to happiness.

Let's get started!

Find a comfortable, relaxed and balanced position. Give yourself permission to be completely present for yourself, and let your body and mind calm down until they become soft and relaxed.

Breathe in, feel relaxed...

breathe out, feel calm...

Breathe in, feel relaxed...

breathe out, feel calm...

Breathe in, feel relaxed...

breathe out, feel calm...

Breathe in, feel relaxed...

breathe out, feel calm...

Allow the mind to distance itself from all thoughts and orientate awareness on your breath. Breathe naturally and do not force a specific rhythm. Let your breath come and go.

Carefully, now, drive your attention from the breath to the space in which you are.

Feel the energy and atmosphere of this space as it permeates all of your being. Notice the noises in the background. Maybe there is a clock ticking, maybe there are cars passing just outside your windows. Whatever you feel it is fine, let your attention rest on the external.

Breathe in, feel relaxed...

breathe out, feel calm...

Breathe in, feel relaxed...

breathe out, feel calm...

Breathe in, feel relaxed...

breathe out, feel calm...

Breathe in, feel relaxed...

breathe out, feel calm...

Now bring the attention back to the breath. Take your time and you will naturally reach a place of warmth and ease. Stay in this state where you feel your body and mind completely calm, relaxed and full of peace for a few minutes, without letting go the focus on your breath.

Breathe in, feel relaxed...

breathe out, feel calm...

Breathe in, feel relaxed...

breathe out, feel calm...

Breathe in, feel relaxed...

breathe out, feel calm...

Breathe in, feel relaxed...

breathe out, feel calm...

Breathe in, feel relaxed...

breathe out, feel calm...

Breathe in, feel relaxed...

breathe out, feel calm...

Breathe in, feel relaxed...

breathe out, feel calm...

Breathe in, feel relaxed...

breathe out, feel calm...

Now that you have reached this deep sense of relaxation, we can begin to shift our focus to the present moment. Allow your mind to naturally sink deeper into the layers of thoughts, until you can start observing everything from a third person perspective.

I will give you a few minutes to do that, as it might take some time for some of you.

Breathe in, feel relaxed...

breathe out, feel calm...

Breathe in, feel relaxed...

breathe out, feel calm...

Breathe in, feel relaxed...

breathe out, feel calm...

Breathe in, feel relaxed...

breathe out, feel calm...

Breathe in, feel relaxed...

breathe out, feel calm...

Breathe in, feel relaxed...

breathe out, feel calm...

Breathe in, feel relaxed...

breathe out, feel calm...

Breathe in, feel relaxed...

breathe out, feel calm...

As you now can see yourself from above, keep following the present moment, grasping everything happening externally and internally. All the emotions arising, all the noises in the background: everything has the same importance and it is worth noticing.

Breathe in, feel relaxed...

breathe out, feel calm...

Breathe in, feel relaxed...

breathe out, feel calm...

Breathe in, feel relaxed...

breathe out, feel calm...

Breathe in, feel relaxed...

breathe out, feel calm...

You may soon realize that everything that comes under your attention, sooner or later leaves your field of mental contact, as something else enters it. This is something worth noting and I will give you a couple of minutes to realize this, as it is the main concept of the entire practice.

Breathe in, feel relaxed...

breathe out, feel calm...

Breathe in, feel relaxed...

breathe out, feel calm...

Breathe in, feel relaxed...

breathe out, feel calm...

Breathe in, feel relaxed...

breathe out, feel calm...

What before was here, now it is not any more and it the space that it created, something else if coming in to fill in the gap. Do not resist the constant and progressive evolution of what you are feeling and perceiving, as it the most basic law of the universe presenting itself to you in its most natural form.

Breathe in, feel relaxed...

breathe out, feel calm...

Breathe in, feel relaxed...

breathe out, feel calm...

Breathe in, feel relaxed...

breathe out, feel calm...

Breathe in, feel relaxed...

breathe out, feel calm...

Breathe in, feel relaxed...

breathe out, feel calm...

Breathe in, feel relaxed...

breathe out, feel calm...

Breathe in, feel relaxed...

breathe out, feel calm...

Breathe in, feel relaxed...

breathe out, feel calm...

The same way noise come and go, the same way your thoughts constantly change, your scars will heal and make place for new beauty and peace. You just need to give yourself time and allow the healing process to take place, without resisting it with your mind.

You do not have to do anything, besides allowing the natural evolution to take place in its most natural form. Evolving means being ready to let go of what no longer serves you and when you will reach the point where you can allow your scars to truly heal, than pain will make space for new positive energy.

Breathe in, feel relaxed...

breathe out, feel calm...

Breathe in, feel relaxed...

breathe out, feel calm...

Breathe in, feel relaxed...

breathe out, feel calm...

Breathe in, feel relaxed...

breathe out, feel calm...

Breathe in, feel relaxed...

breathe out, feel calm...

Breathe in, feel relaxed...

breathe out, feel calm...

Breathe in, feel relaxed...

breathe out, feel calm...

Breathe in, feel relaxed...

breathe out, feel calm...

Just keep noticing everything that goes on inside and outside you. It can be useful to label each thing with a name. For example, whenever you feel a thought arising, you can say "thought" inside your head. This will help you look at things from a third person perspective, without judging what you are feeling.

Breathe in, feel relaxed...

breathe out, feel calm...

Breathe in, feel relaxed...

breathe out, feel calm...

Breathe in, feel relaxed...

breathe out, feel calm...

Breathe in, feel relaxed...

breathe out, feel calm...

Breathe in, feel relaxed...

breathe out, feel calm...

Breathe in, feel relaxed...

breathe out, feel calm...

Breathe in, feel relaxed...

breathe out, feel calm...

Breathe in, feel relaxed...

breathe out, feel calm...

Keep noticing and labelling, as this process reinforces the idea that everything is here to go away and that change is the only true constant. Now you have thoughts, now you have noises, now you are scared, now you have courage. It is a never ending cycle of "things" and we are here to witness this marvellous show unfolding in front of our very own eyes.

Breathe in, feel relaxed...

breathe out, feel calm...

Breathe in, feel relaxed...

breathe out, feel calm...

Breathe in, feel relaxed...

breathe out, feel calm...

Breathe in, feel relaxed...

breathe out, feel calm...

Breathe in, feel relaxed...

breathe out, feel calm...

Breathe in, feel relaxed...

breathe out, feel calm...

Breathe in, feel relaxed...

breathe out, feel calm...

Breathe in, feel relaxed...

breathe out, feel calm...

I will give you a few more minutes to focus on this, before reaching the end of our session.

Breathe in, feel relaxed...

breathe out, feel calm...

Breathe in, feel relaxed...

breathe out, feel calm...

Breathe in, feel relaxed...

breathe out, feel calm...

Breathe in, feel relaxed...

breathe out, feel calm...

Breathe in, feel relaxed...

breathe out, feel calm...

Breathe in, feel relaxed...

breathe out, feel calm...

Breathe in, feel relaxed...

breathe out, feel calm...

Breathe in, feel relaxed...

breathe out, feel calm...

Breathe in, feel relaxed…

breathe out, feel calm…

Breathe in, feel relaxed…

breathe out, feel calm…

Breathe in, feel relaxed…

breathe out, feel calm…

Breathe in, feel relaxed…

breathe out, feel calm…

Breathe in, feel relaxed…

breathe out, feel calm…

Breathe in, feel relaxed…

breathe out, feel calm…

Breathe in, feel relaxed…

breathe out, feel calm…

Breathe in, feel relaxed…

breathe out, feel calm...

Now bring the attention back to the body and start feeling your arms and legs once again. You can close your hands or move your fingers, just to take control of the space around you.

Please, keep the eyes closed for now and enjoy the beautiful moment you are living. You have given yourself the time to feel better and that is absolutely incredible.

Breathe in, feel relaxed...

breathe out, feel calm...

Breathe in, feel relaxed...

breathe out, feel calm...

Breathe in, feel relaxed...

breathe out, feel calm...Breathe in, feel relaxed...

breathe out, feel calm...

Now become aware of the environment around you once again. Feel the different sounds, the temperature of the room you are in and once you are ready, open the eyes again.

www.ingramcontent.com/pod-product-compliance
Lightning Source LLC
Chambersburg PA
CBHW071840080526
44589CB00012B/1074